In Stillness

Penny Reilly

ISBN 978-0-99224759-6-3

Cover art, "In Stillness" Penny Reilly
Interior images, mixed fine-art and
photography, poetry and text, Penny Reilly
Text Editor, Rosalie Franklin

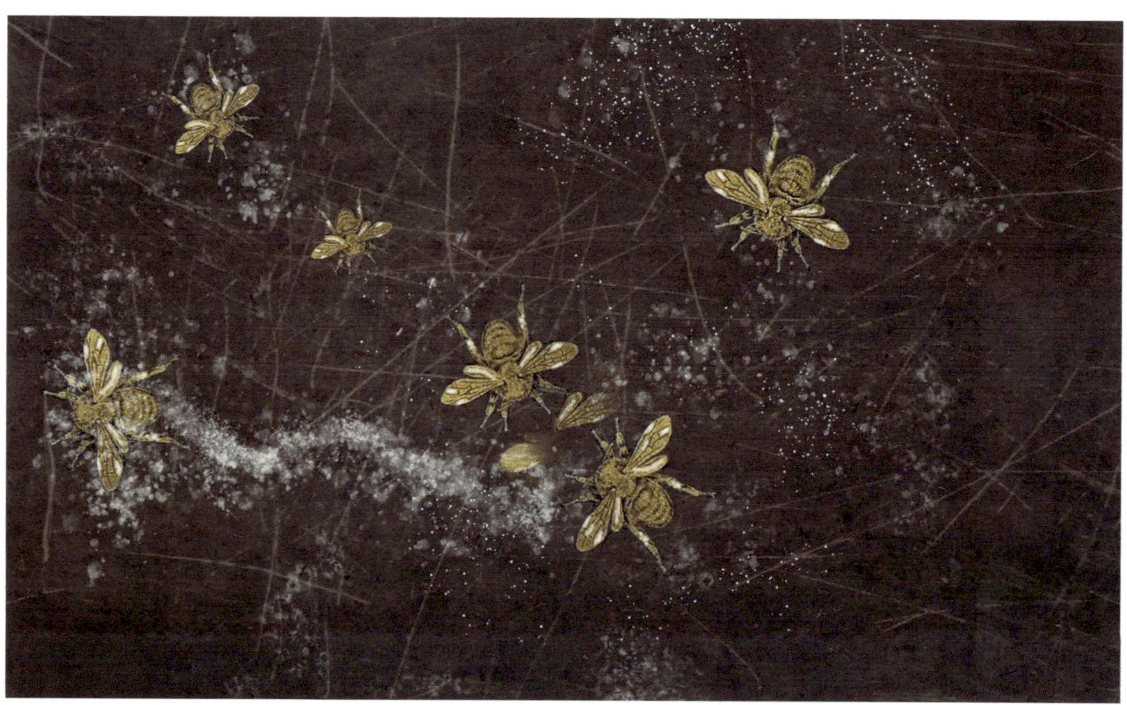

Transition... mixed media fine art... Penny Reilly 2018

Who Did It?

The world slept
A waxing moon kept
watch in the sky
The sun rose
from a hazy doze
Night froze
in the sky
One moment there
then the sky was bare
Who stole the moon
Who did it
And so she left
our souls bereft
...like a spark she flew
in the night sky
Now another star shines bright
but who stole her gentle light
...our moon
from the sky

...for Suzie, always...

Dedication

I offer this book in memory of Suzie Reilly, 1971-2018

Daughter, sister, friend,
taken far too early.
Always with me
and forever young.

Introduction...

Penny Reilly presents a small collection of mixed-media work that express sadness, in and for, the world she sees. Through a re-connection with the essence of her inspiration... Nature, in both imagery and words, she is offering a solution.

Reilly is a UK born published author, photographer, poet and artist. She moved to Australia in 1980 and currently resides in the Daylesford region of Victoria.

Well-known for photography, art and written works, this is her first mixed-media exhibition of combined, subtly tectured layers of fine-art photography, ink and water colour palette

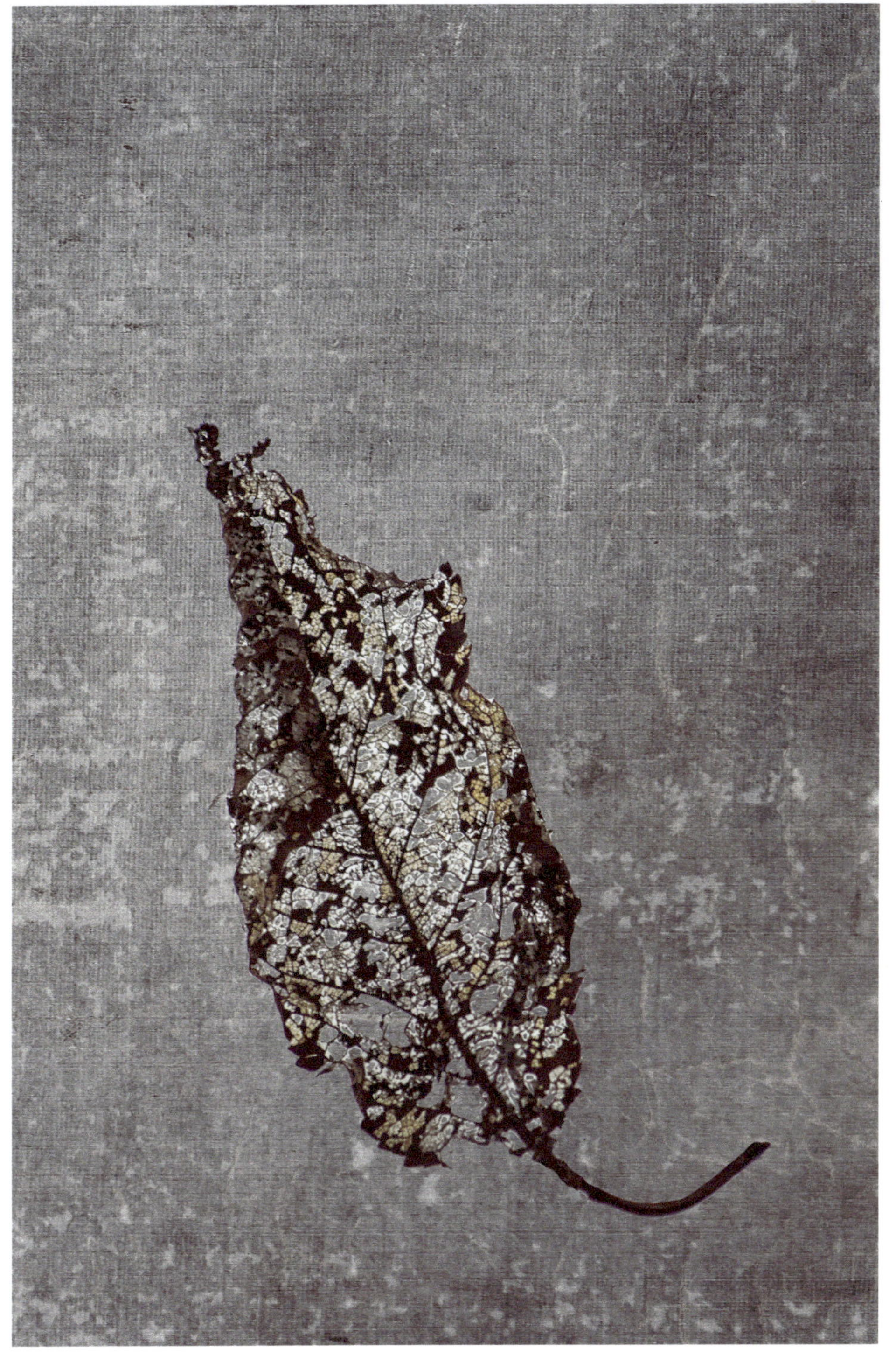

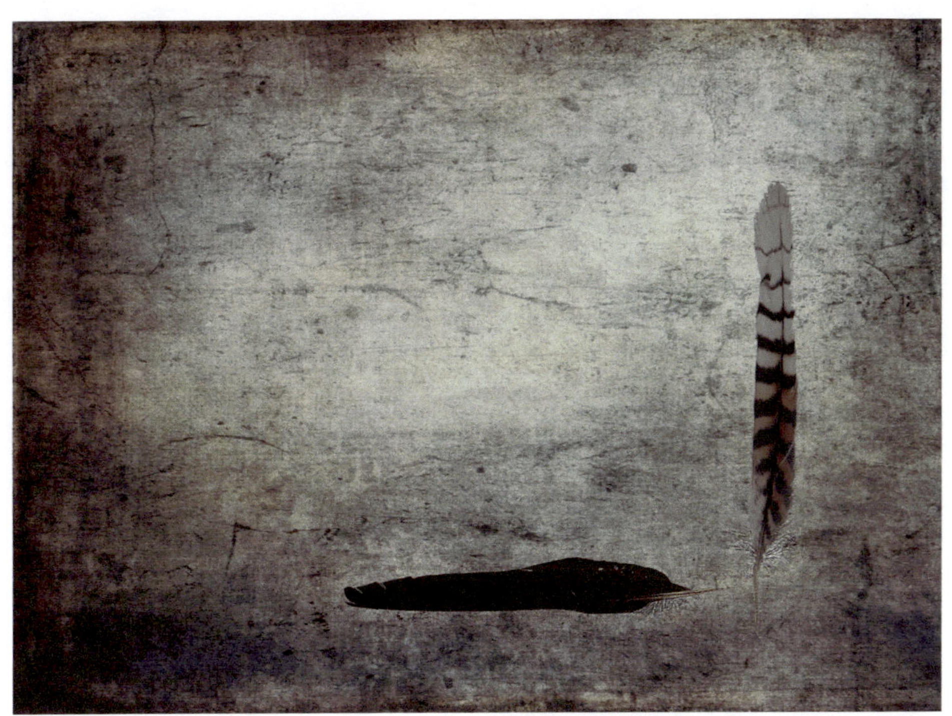

Penny Reilly...

'Nature will always win, because the falling away of identity is not judged. One cell in a single leaf, reflects the whole leaf - the whole tree, which in turn, reflects every tree in the species, across our planet, communicating the condition of their entire species, to those who hear... thus honouring ancestry.'

PR, 2019

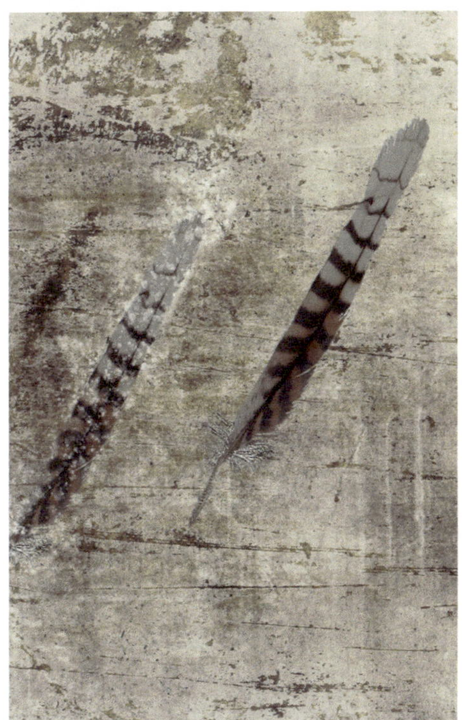

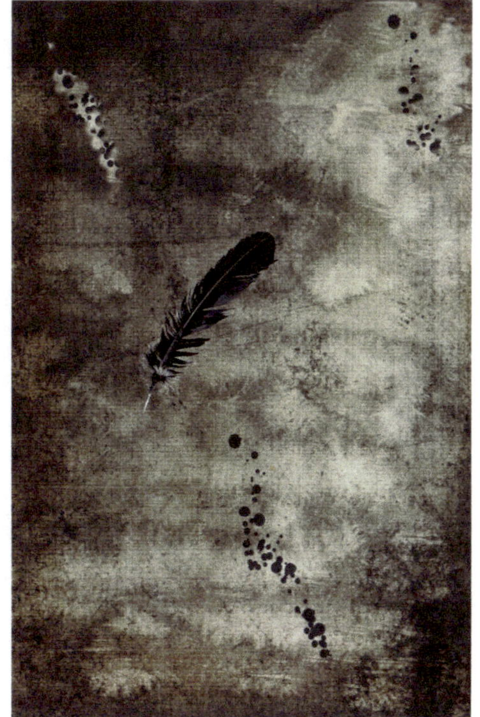

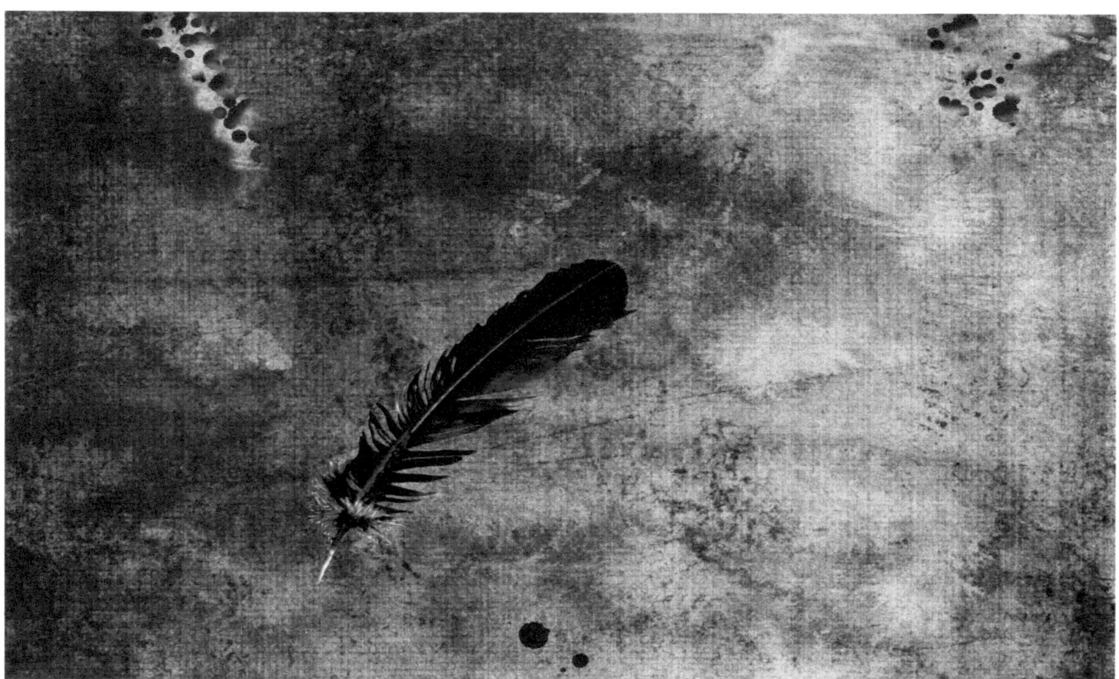

Between
the rustling of leaves
when spent is the breeze
...lies the sound of silence
Between
one breath and the next
a pause... an apex
...lies the sound of silence
Between
each beat of a heart
from the first, to the last
...lies the sound of silence
Between
each blink of an eye
with sights set on an empty sky
..lies the sound of silence
Between
white noise...
a black void
Between
red crackling flames...
speaking in tongues
crying your name
Between
a songbird's lilt
the sound
between each notes
that tilt your world
into sound
...or silence

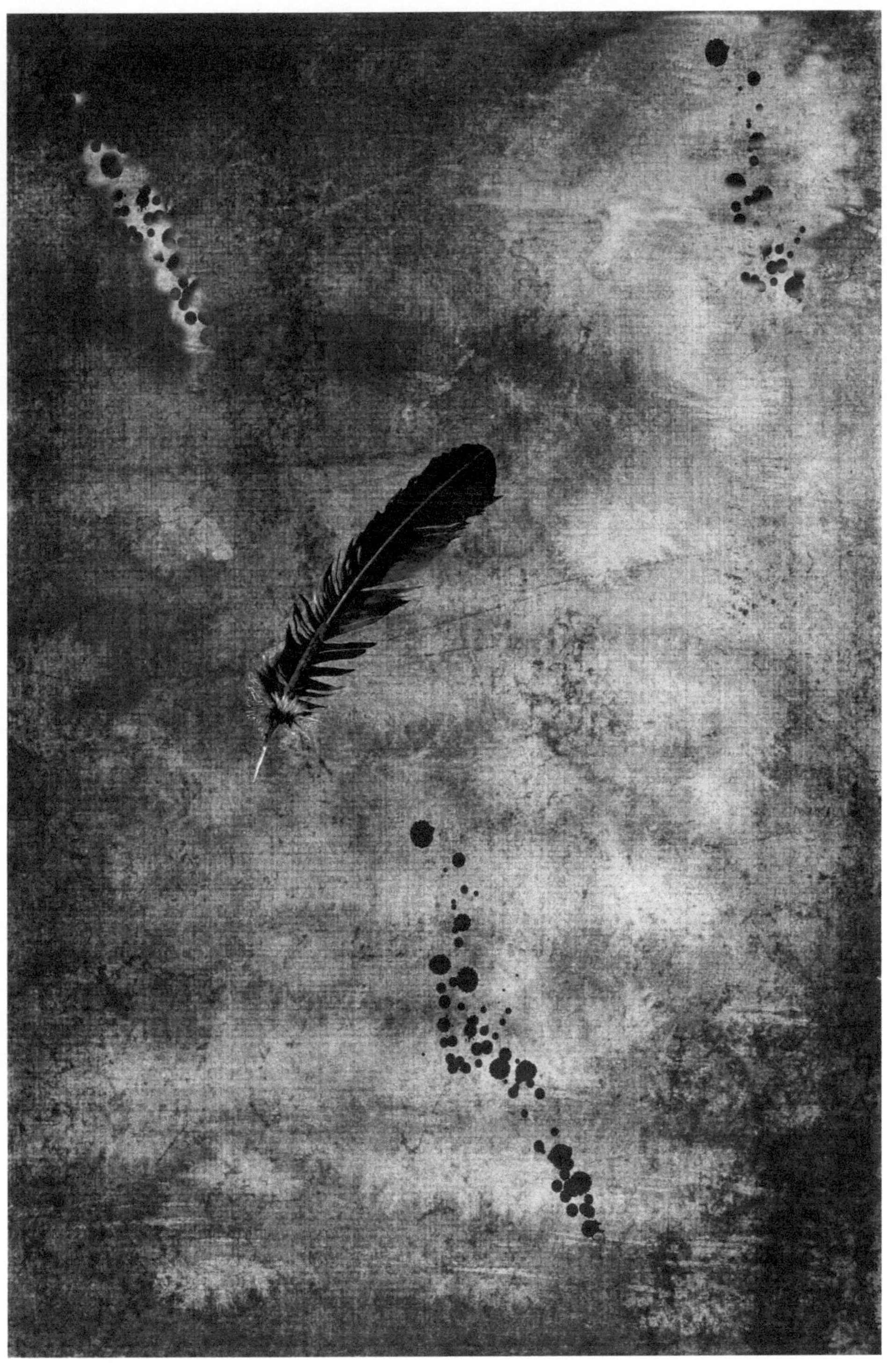

Shift...

I felt a shift...
Deeper this time
...a quickening
...a connection
to merge with the planet
to give her multifaceted life
to give her a physical voice
and then I knew...
she already is
and we already are
we just have to remember
our roots
our intrinsic ancestry
Her waters, our blood
Her grass-covered earth, our skin
Her rocks and peaks, our bones
and be her in every wild sense
fiercely, passionately
through every reemerging
...wild, spidery-sense

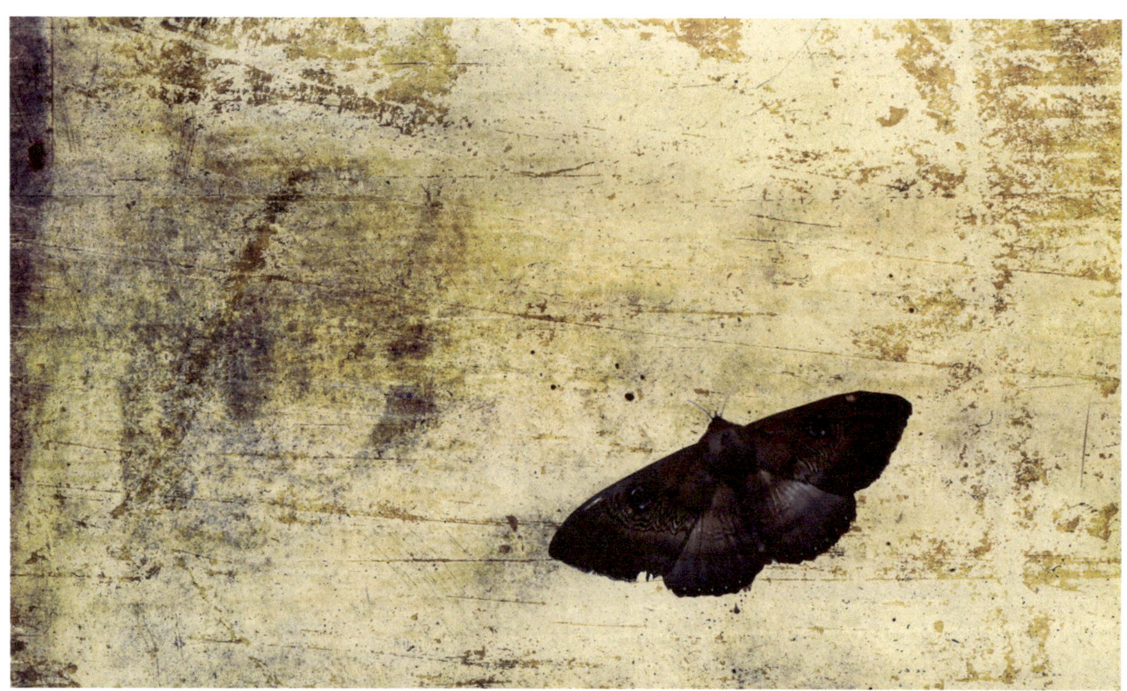

Eternal Flight...

Life
A tapestry of discarded things
Moth and dragon fly wings
Autumn leaves aglow
with russet tones
A forgotten creatures' bones
that now, in stillness sing
...of eternal flight

What calls us
in the dämmerung
What tiny tributes
gut wrenching
heart hammering
yield to us a moment
...a tiny insight
of a life
that now, in stillness sings
...of eternal flight

What tales
along dappled path
by sun-bathed stream
give us a moments pause
...of another's dream
In honouring this
indeed
in their last rite
that now, in stillness sings
...of eternal flight

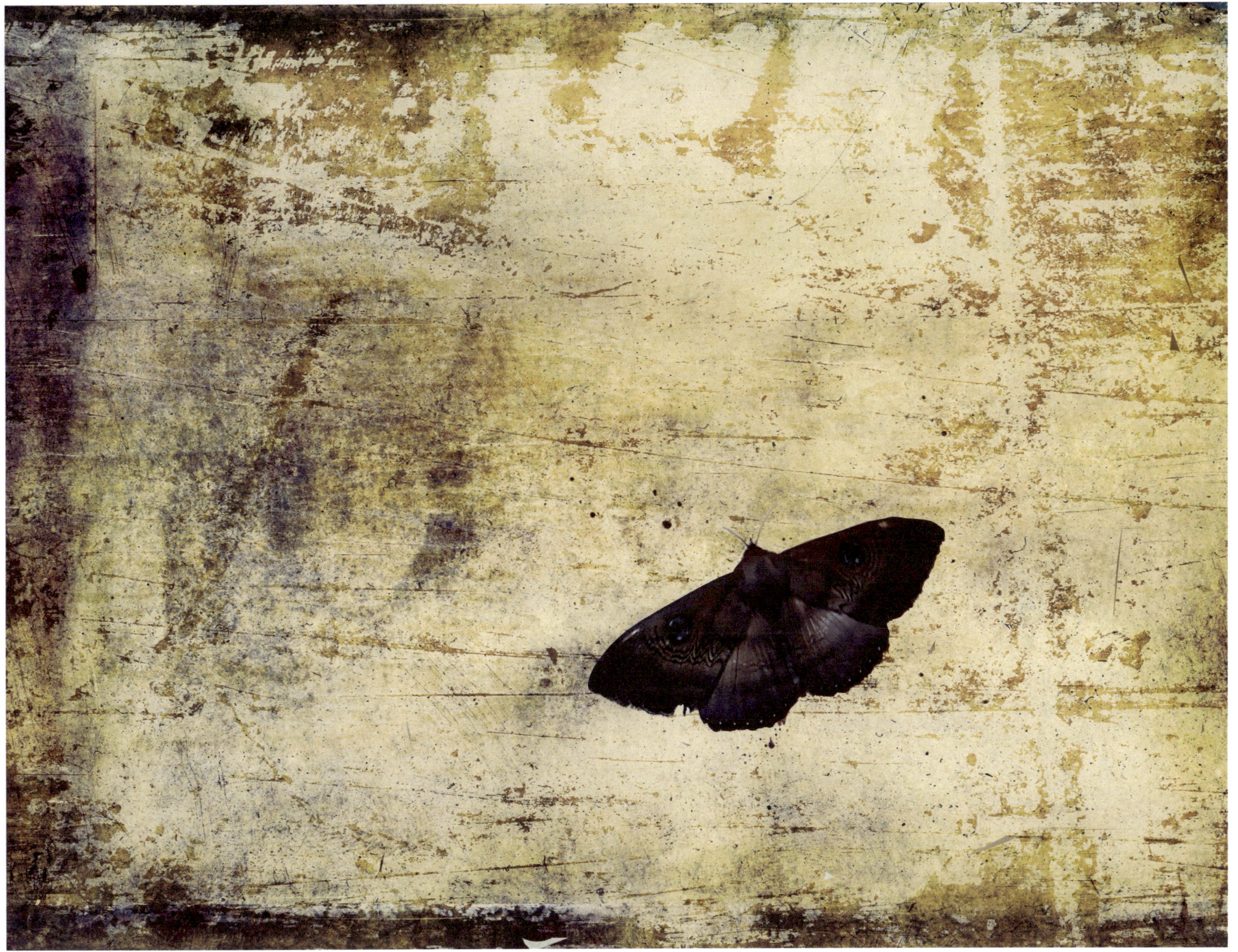

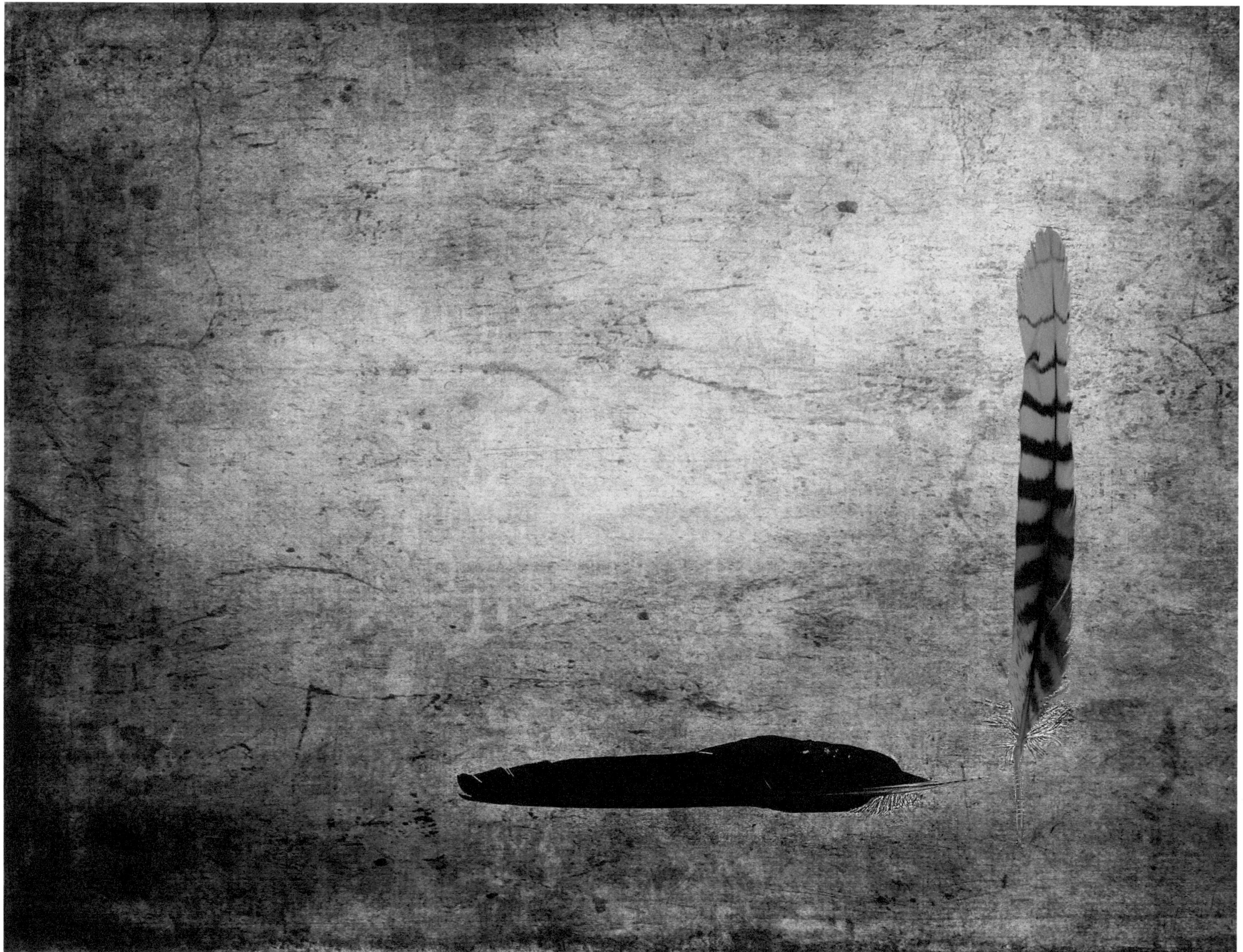

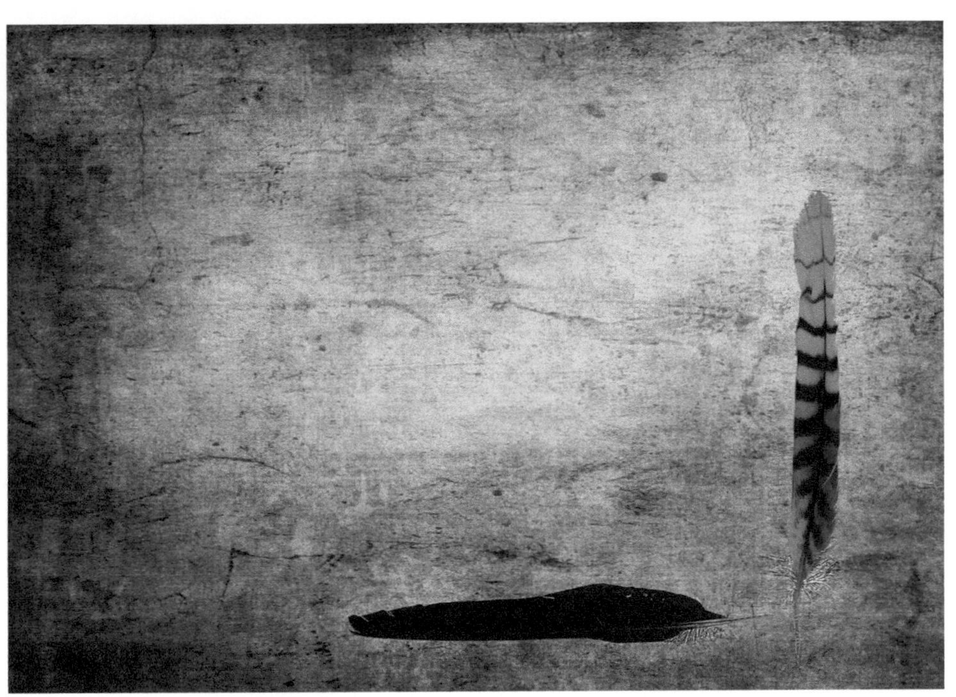

We all experience
times in our life
Naturally occurring periods
in any life-cycle
when we fail to understand
that endings are precursors
to new beginnings
When our life-rhythms
move us into, and through
those dark times
We can be ignorant
of what is happening
except with the benefit of hindsight
and that it is
in actuality
a time of mystery
wisdom
...and healing power

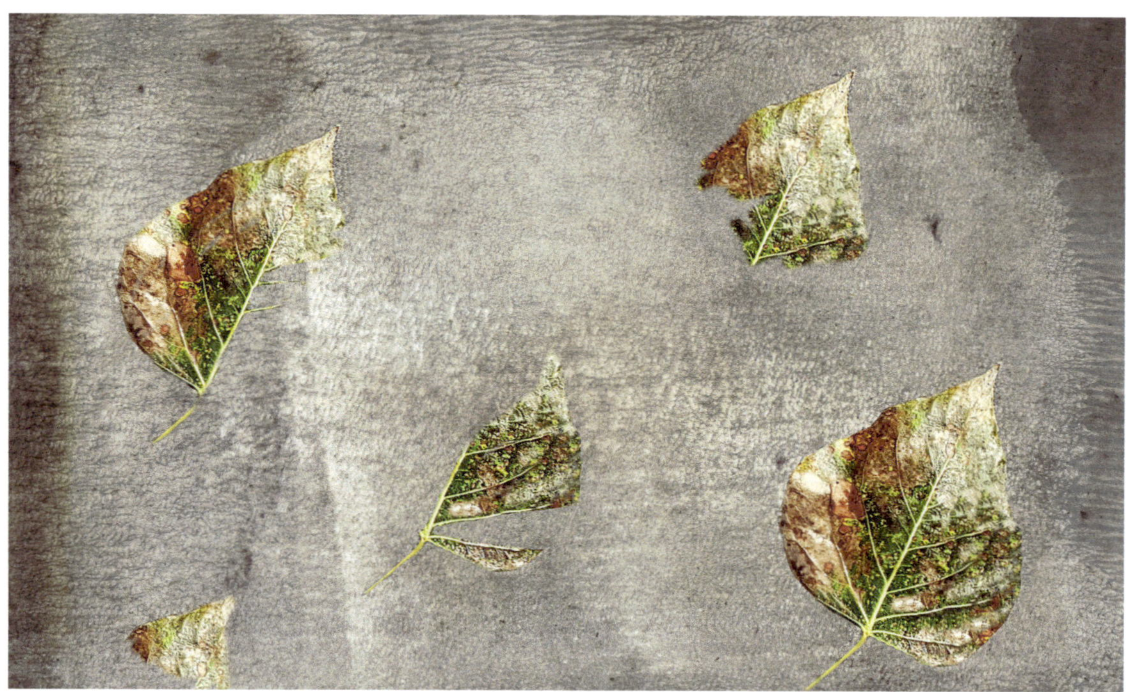

Ripped Apart...

Ripped apart
Raggedy ends laid bare
Where do I start
down the road that leads
to self-repair
It will emerge
I see those tell-tale signs
as long as I tread carefully
between the heart
and life-lines
She will always be close
walking with me
along that healing path
Laughter stirring my soul
giggling as we did
daughter, sister, friend
That is the road
that does not end
and, will take me
in hope, one day
at least, to almost-whole
The trick is
to leave the empty spaces unfilled
Not filled with minutia
With raw processes
...undistilled
Let the truth ferment
Let the joy of knowing
be the balm to heal the pain
And my thoughts will stray, in time
...along the path to peace again

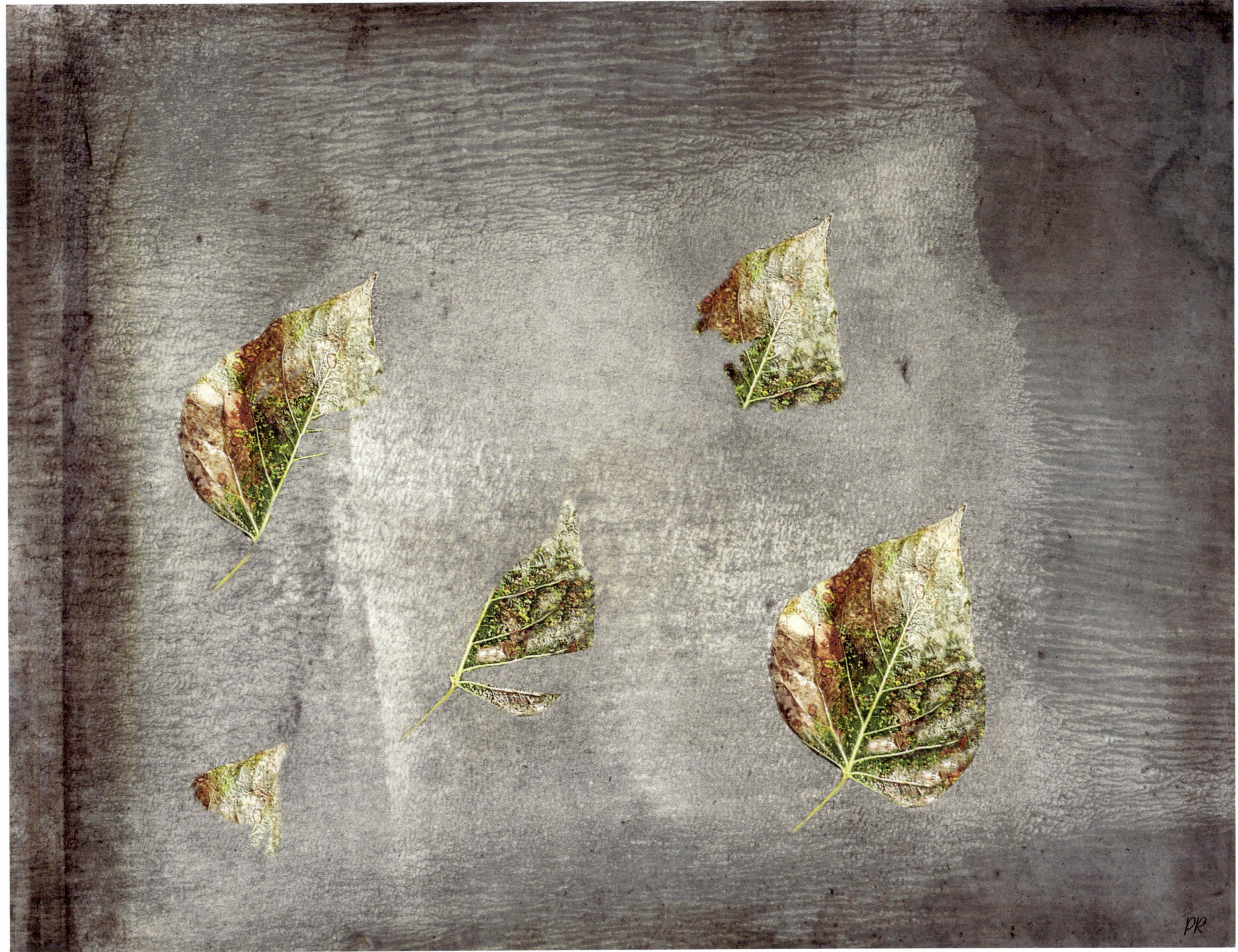
PR

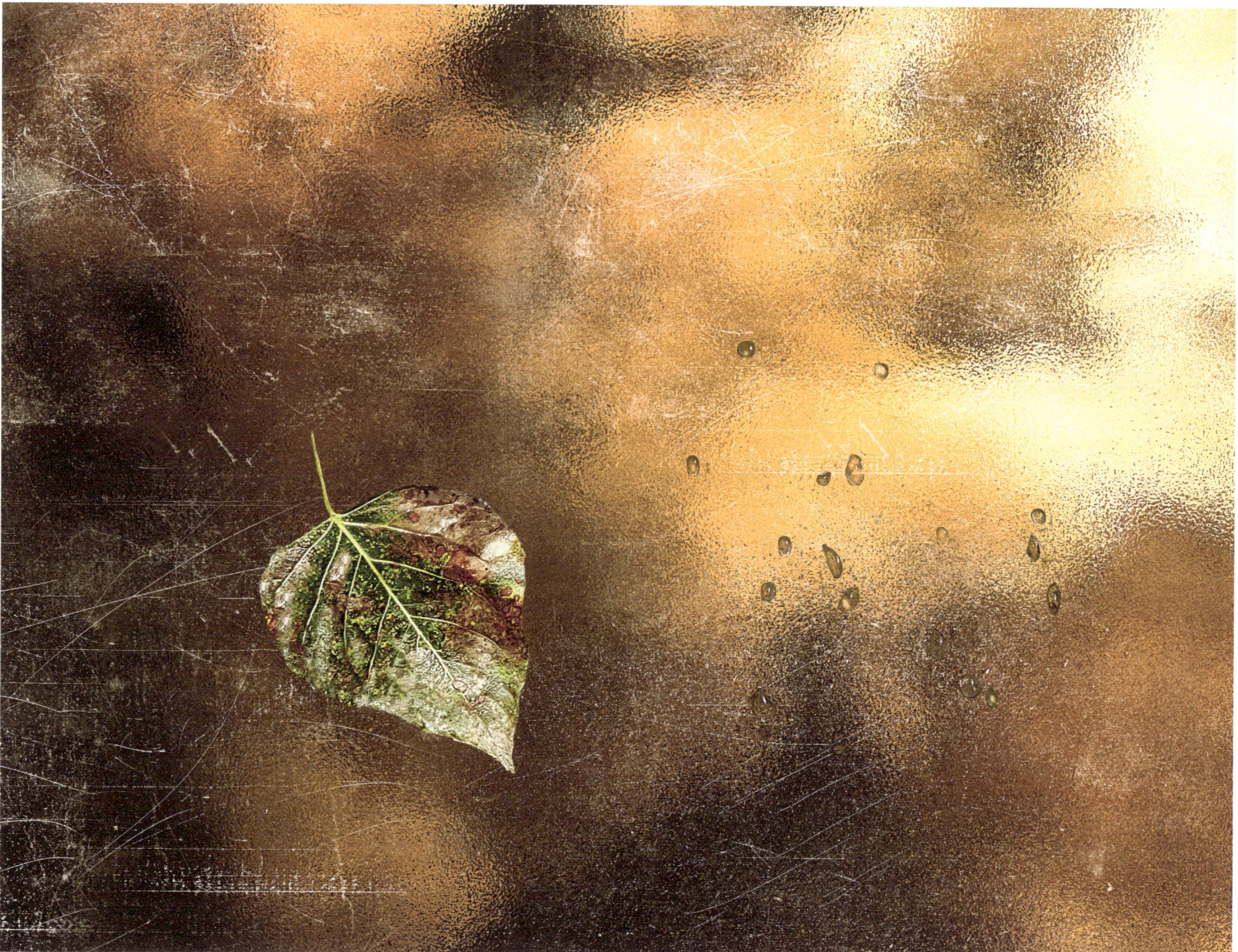

Song of Light...

Coloured prisms
Vibrating rhythms
Fleck the inside of my eyes
with light
Auras, jewell-bright
Exquisite heat
in a throbbing beat
of ancient song
Gaelic. Latin, Greek
in coloured tones embossed
Chapels, echo with sound
A monk's multi-toned drone
A weeping cello
Pagan horns, bellow
in Oak Groves
In the shadows
under monolithic stones
In a cairn of bone
where haunting voices strain
toward the light
Gentle
Mellow
In languages lost
Dark
cannot exist
in any tongue
when healing songs are sung
even on the darkest night
for without the dark
...we cannot see the light

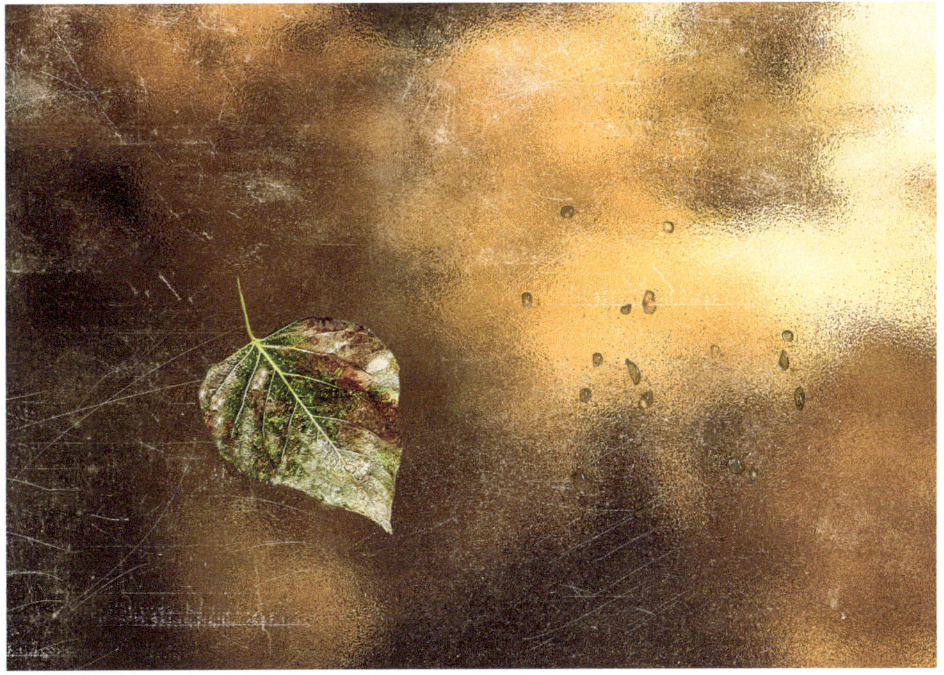

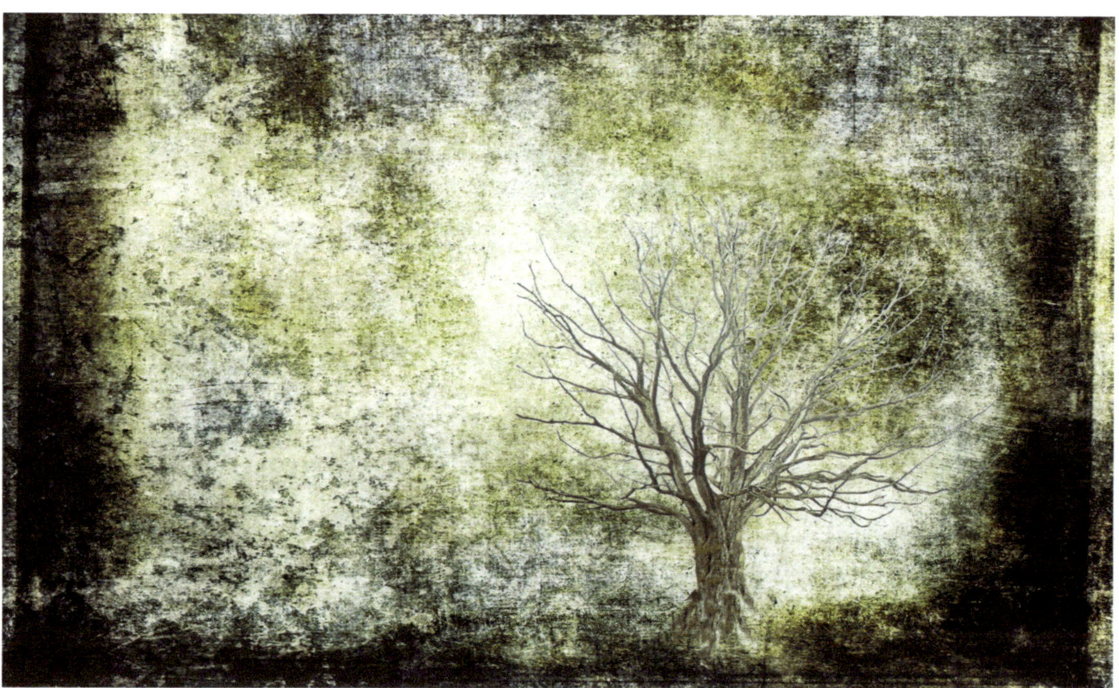

Faded...

Winter, the season
Winter in my heart
Faded, empty spaces
while tendrils
ready to burst-bud
wither, green-faded
Longing for Spring
like birds flying
to foreign places
caught in a net
or on a sword
Double-edged
Sharp-bladed
Spring will come
She will find her way
back from the deep
hollowed-out self
Always searching
even in sleep
for a fresh
unclouded day
to bring back the sun
Telling the wind
to sweep
...to nest
in the warm places
...of a summer-filled heart

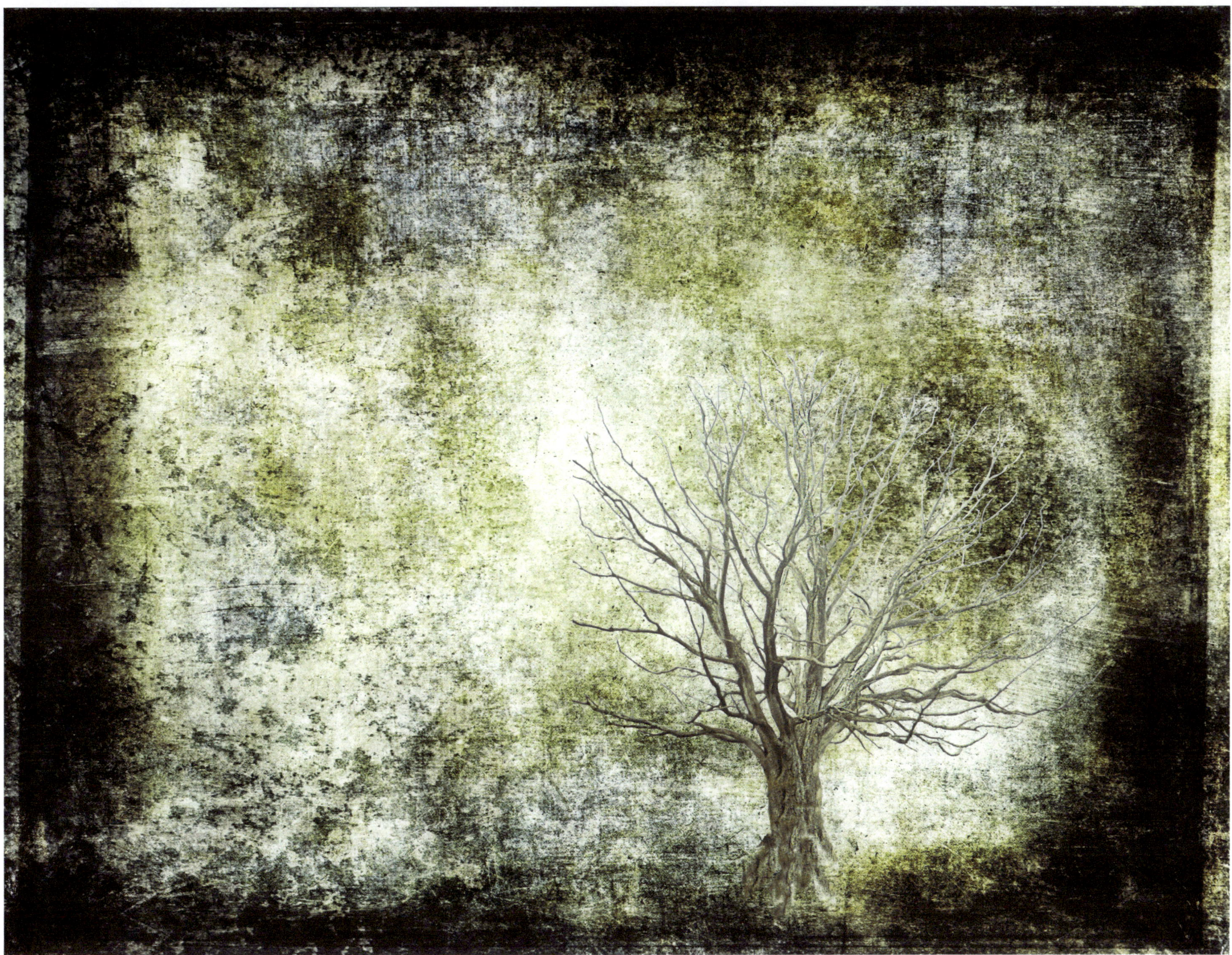

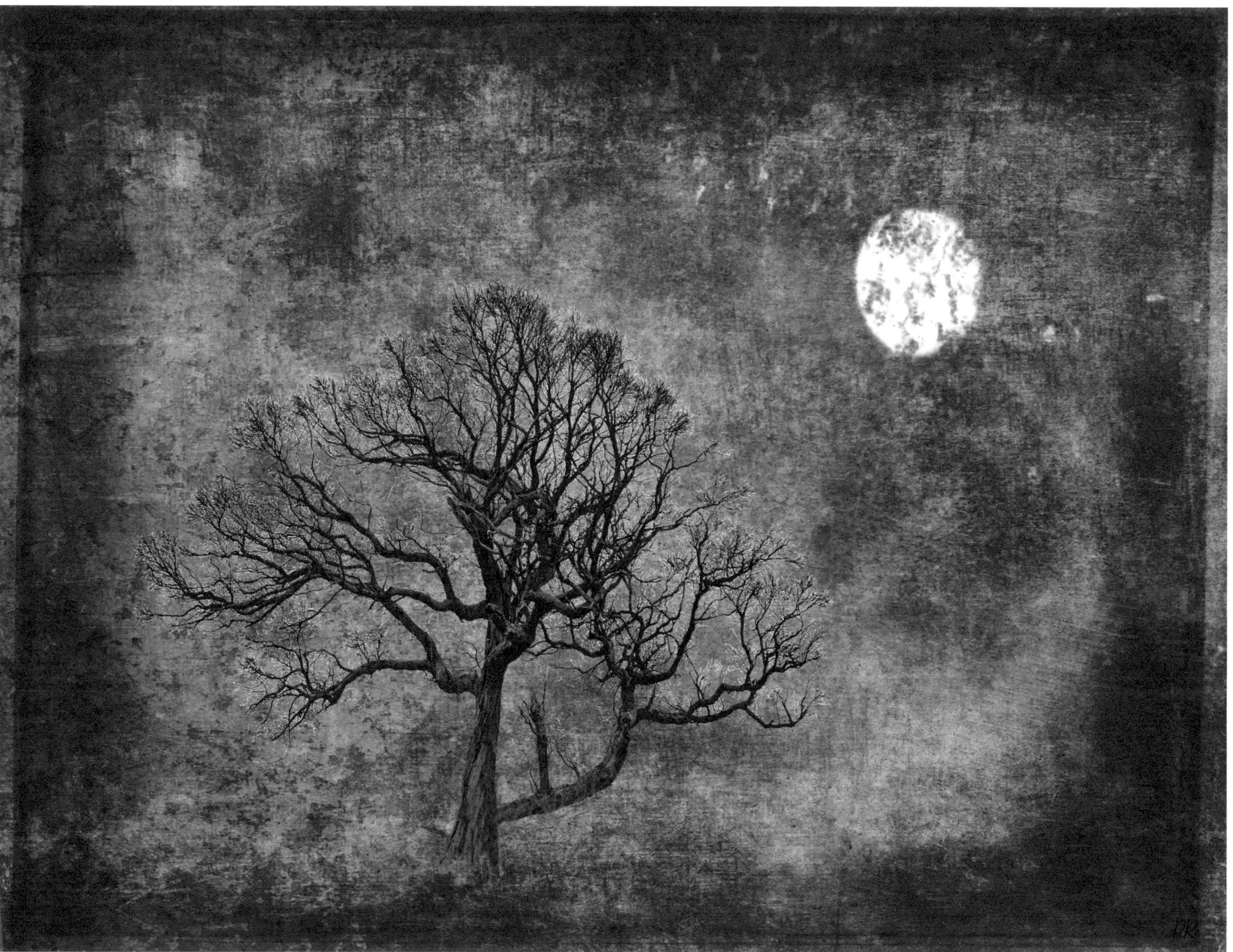

Up-thrusting...

Deep within the earth
a seedling sprouts
Bursting through soil crust
with a silent shout
Does the rhythmic pressure
of unfolding days
create a harmonic movement
an intrigue
that inward plays
its note
of music barely heard
A natural way of being
most miss
Sunlight and moonlight
conjoined
in an ancient kiss
How absurd
that what gives us breath
is seen as untoward
but
if we seek
deeper yet
no intrigue will beget
...spring
Nature up-thrusting
through fragrant
...greeening sward

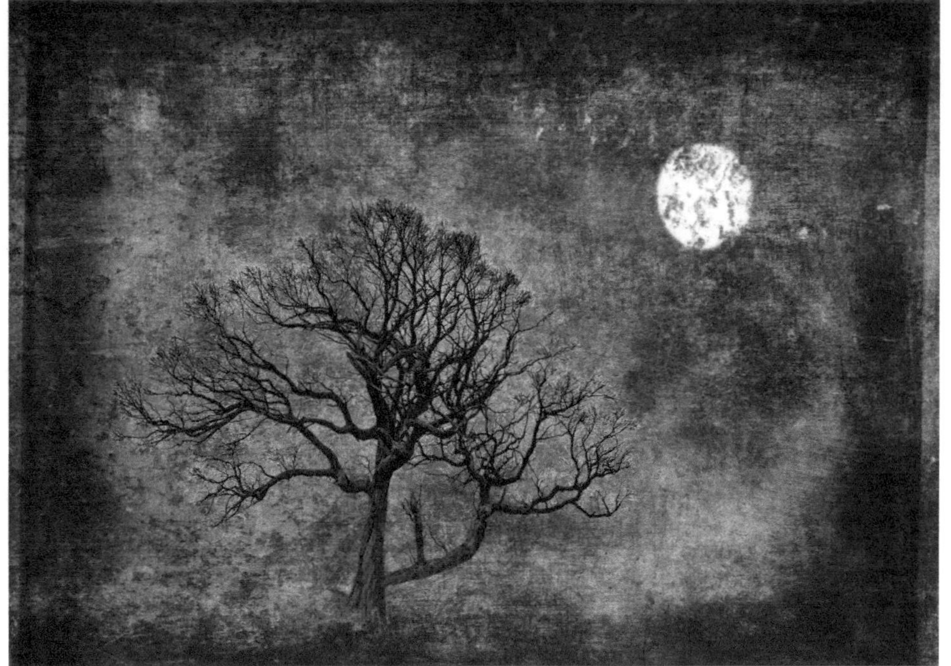

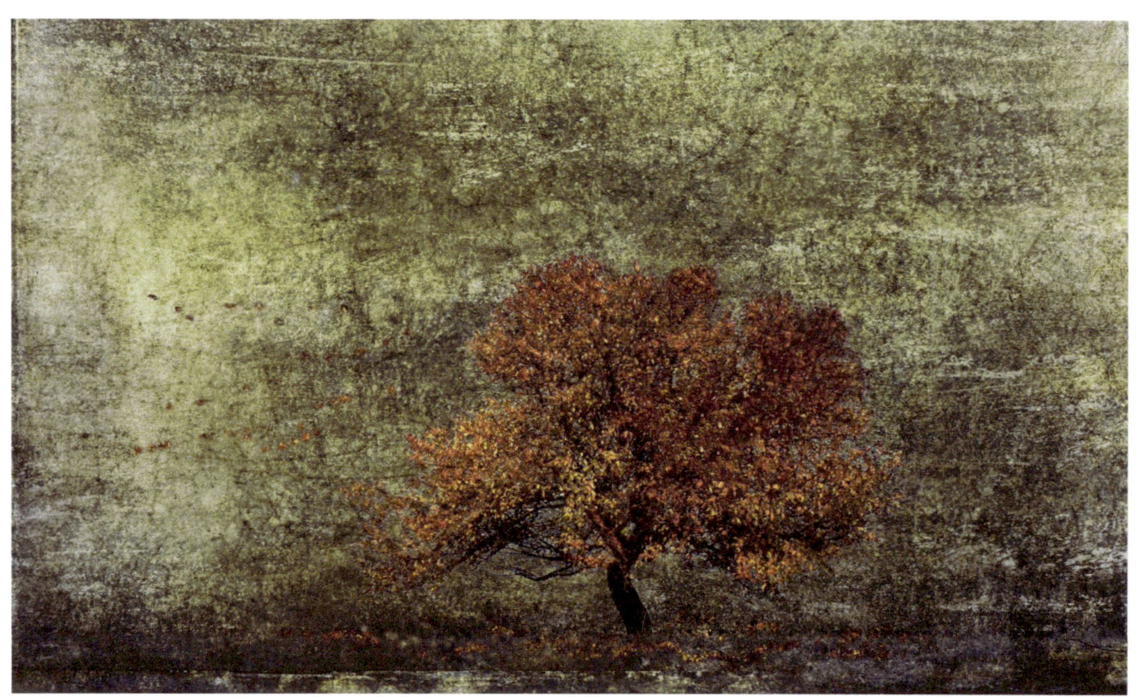

Light Flow...

Light flows
in stillness
behind my eyes
Colour glows
in rhythmic pulsing
Shadows flee
Wild energies encompass
the depths of me
where music swells
Satin notes
Celestial bells
Fear and care dissolve
All senses involve
in subtle warmth
of autumnal light
I dare
to merge
what, perceivably
separate was
from All That Is
...with all there is of me

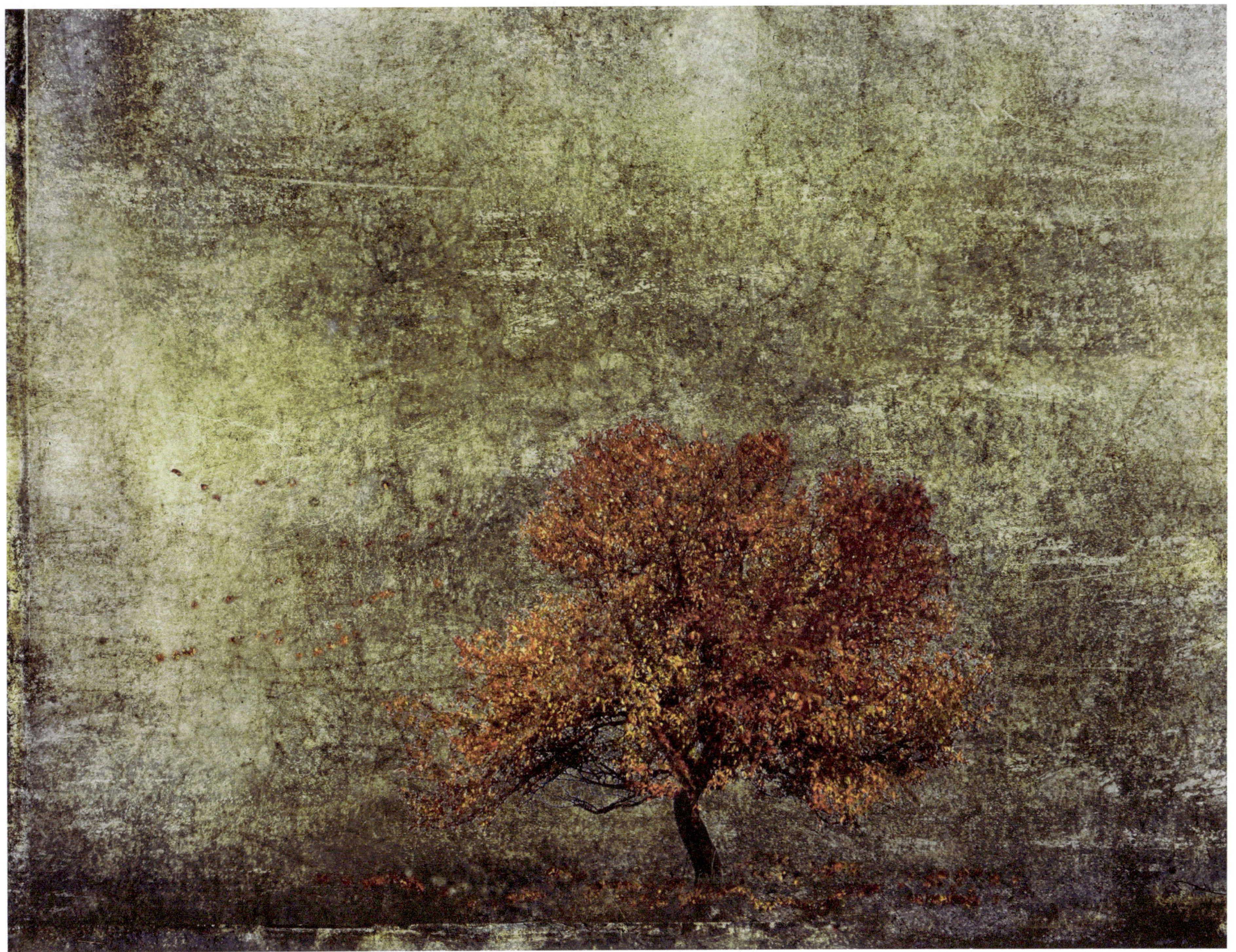

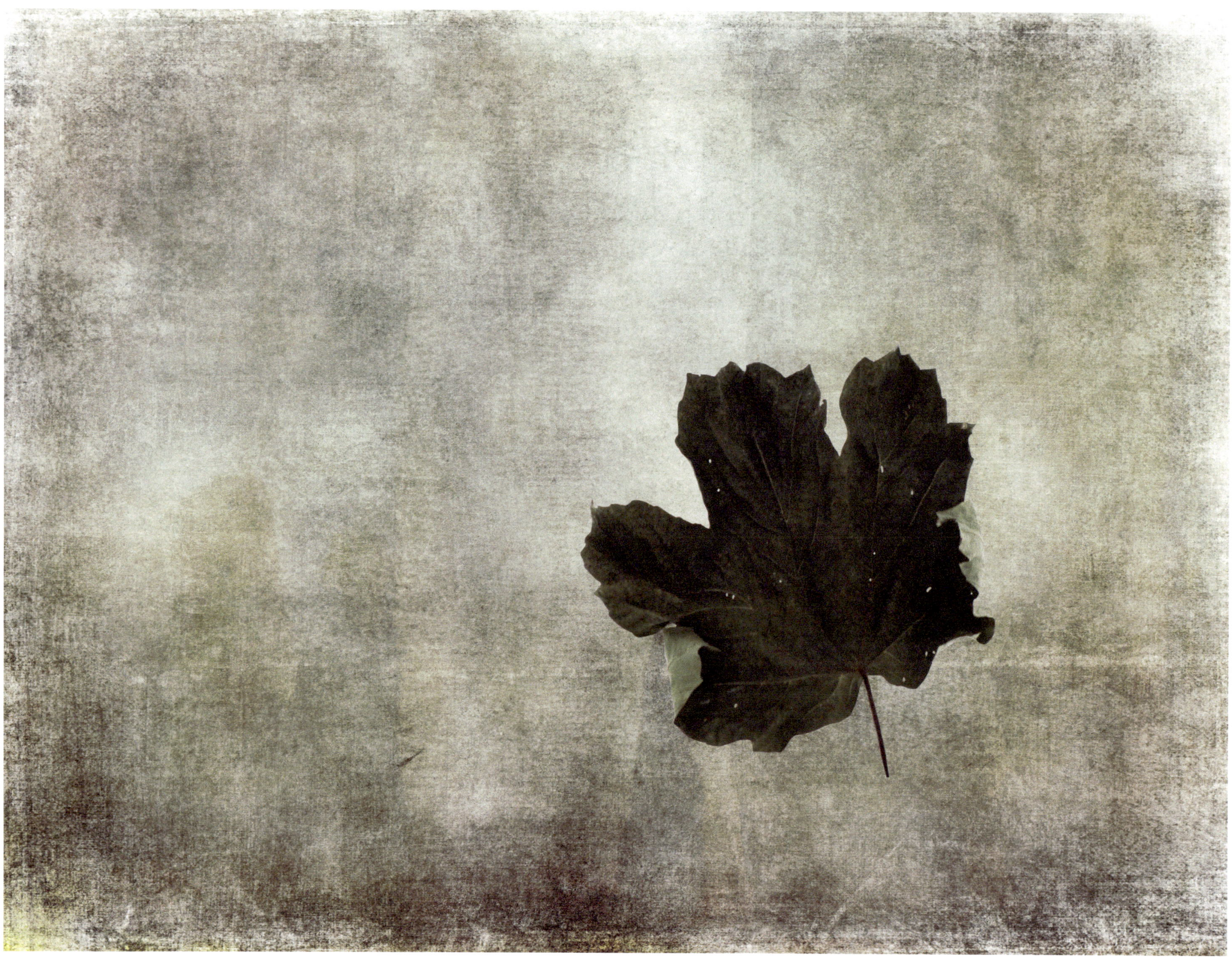

Wild Places...

Wild places
in our heart
Fuelled by joy and pain
in equal measure
Fear and pleasure
Wild places
Woodland ways
offering solitude
and peace
for all our days
Wild places
Wind-blown nights
of surging powers
hiding secret lights
in codes of ancient memory
written in the dark
In the
Wild places
...of our heart

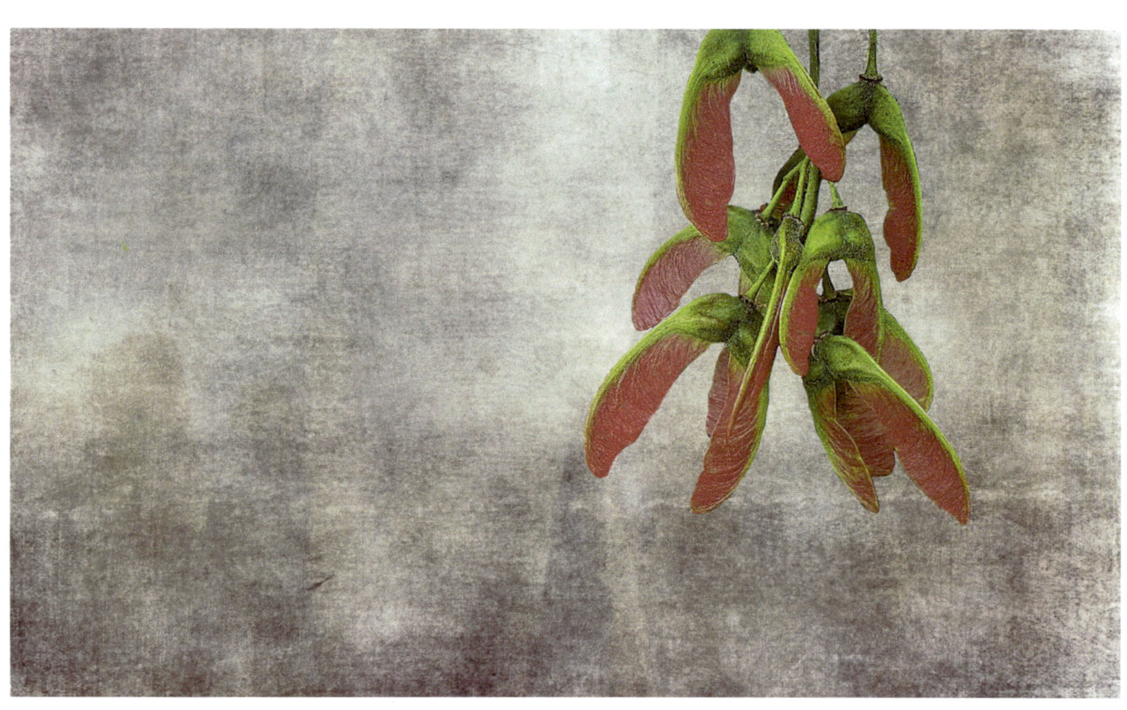

Life is awareness
Layers of being
Birth to death
Seeing
Renewal of life
Excepting
all things pass
Some
wide-eyed
on sweet
green grass
Effortlessly
fearlessly
the last breath's hiss
releasing
a sweet soul-kiss
...all can learn from this

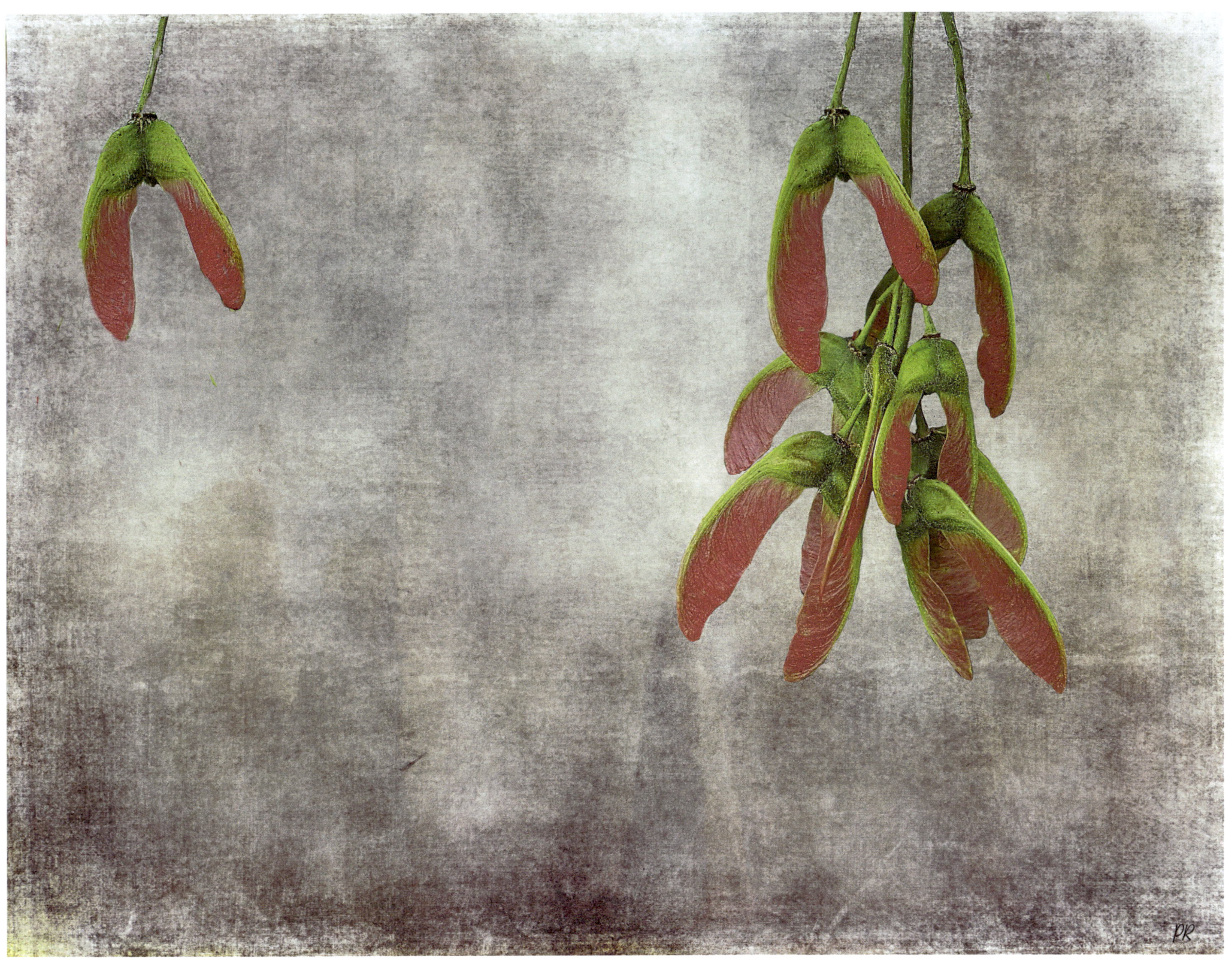

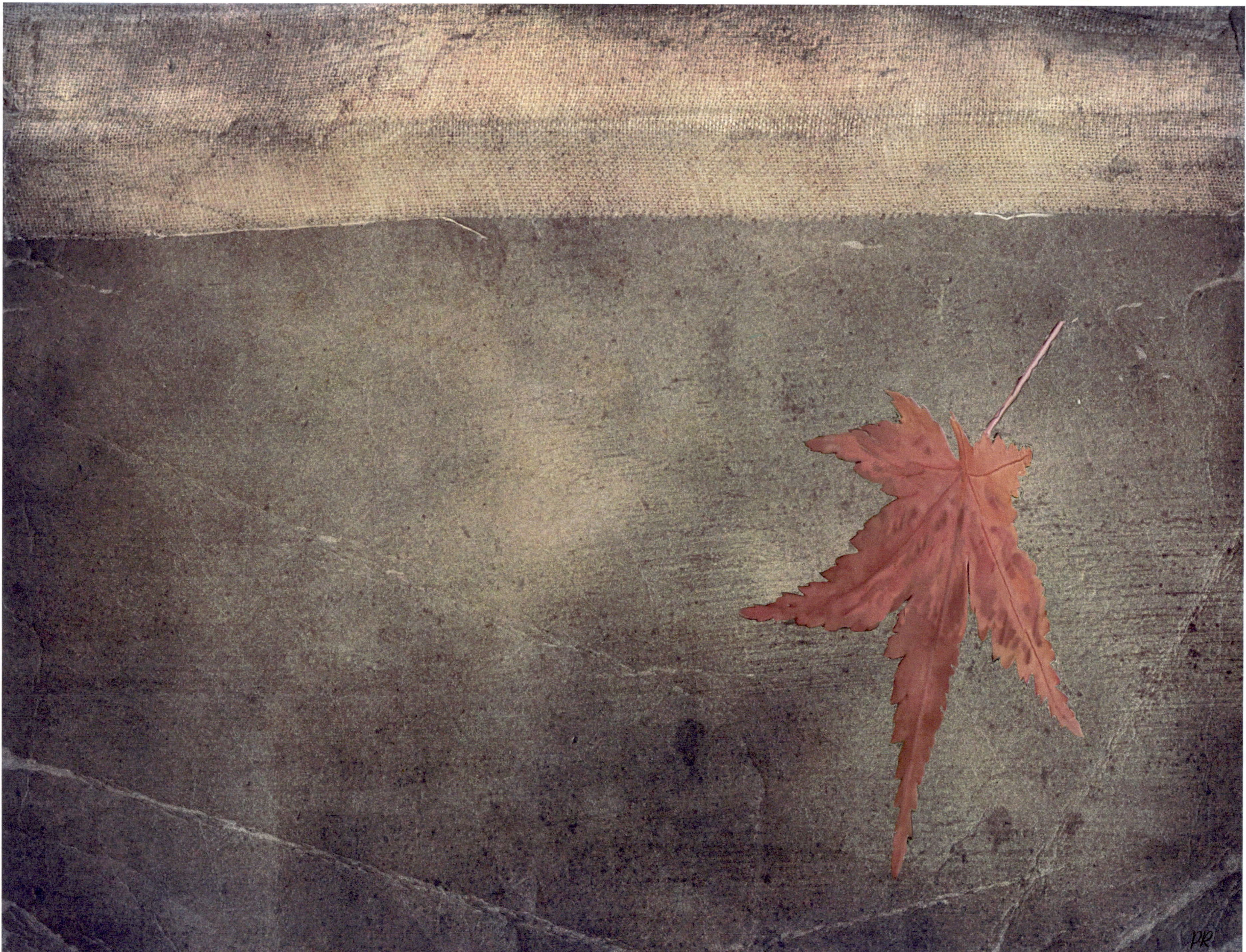

Focus...

Don't focus on the world of lies
Focus on the jewel-bright skies
On nature's day or glorious night
In equal measure, dark and light
Don't let the fear of a distant gun
disturb the rhythm
of your heartbeat drum
Don't stress the days, you fear might come
...for fearing brings them closer

Mankind is lost in many ways
lead by oligarchs bound to enslave
...your thoughts
Herding cells into lab retorts
Giving importance to status
and percentage reports
while a minority dine in swanky resorts
and others drown in oily ports
...wanting only freedom

Focus on the seasons, each in turn
One cycle, not more relevant
...although often you may yearn
for warmth in winter - cool in summer days
yet, each brings a bounty, its own unique ways
Be aware, every thought you weave
A sigh, a sob, for all you grieve
brings into reality what you believe
...for you to stumble over

Focus on the earth-skin geen
On bursting bud... on rushing stream
and the balance there, makes you free
...keeps you strong
Seek the beauty of your planet
Listen only to her song
Be awake, be aware of where your focus lies
On pain or fear, life or death
...or pristine waters, and jewel-bright skies

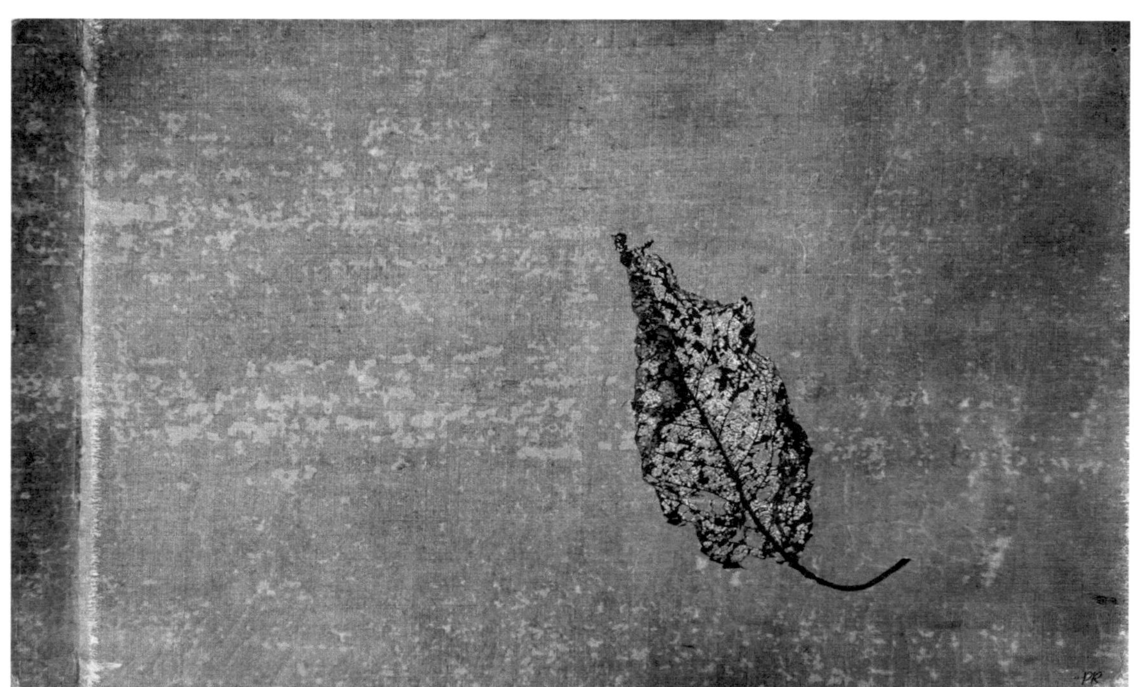

Rush...

Don't rush
into your day
Don't push
long-held dreams
away
for all the
should do
could do
Leaving no space
for you
Be aware
...dare
to say no
Be in awe
as winter thaw
runs
in rivulets
of melting snow
and bees drone
their spring-song
silent
for cold months long
Don't wait
Live the moment fully
as if there were
...nowhere else to go

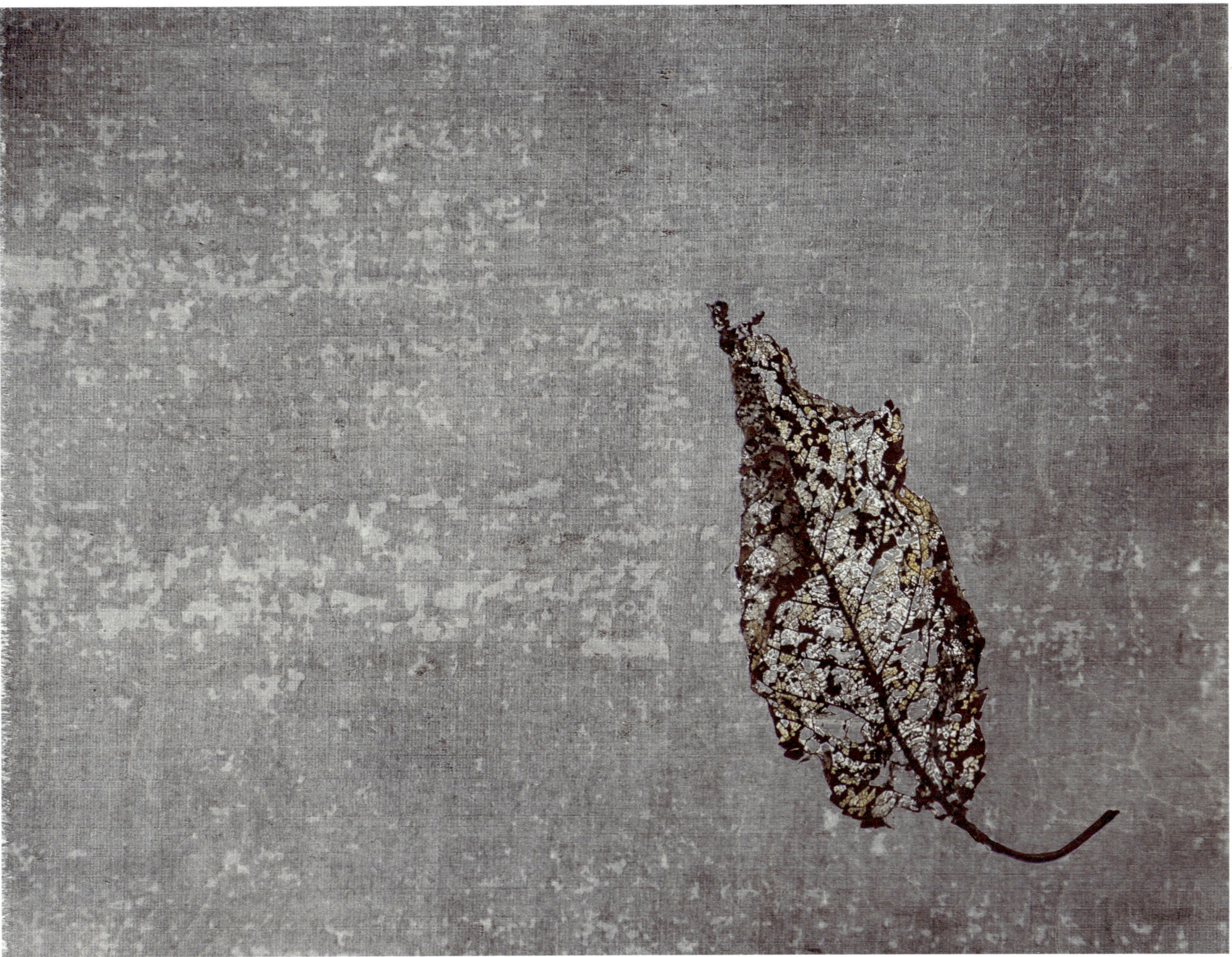

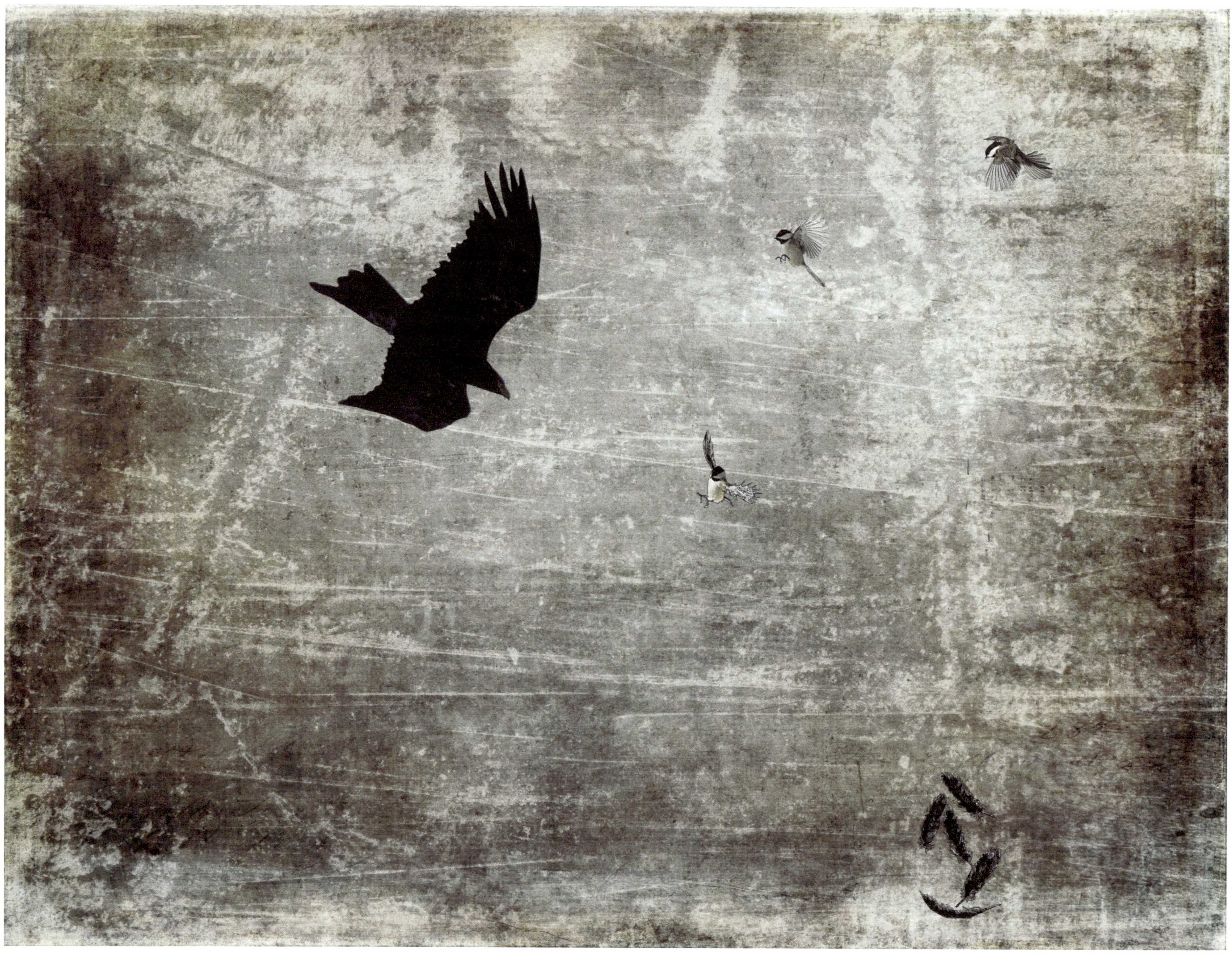

A Breath of Timelessness...

No straight lines here
in timeless space
Only spinning
spiralling threads
...secrets hid
in glowing grace
In musing
without judgement
all things become removed
If I were lost
would my seeking-self
become unglued
from substance
in seeking
the essence of my truth
And in that search
would that very essence
be my proof
that in eternity
is found
...not loss
but subtle gain
Finding in a moment
all that holds my joy
...my pain
for what is one
without the other seen
A secret only
A spark of consciousness
A breath of timelessness
in a troubled world
...is all I've been

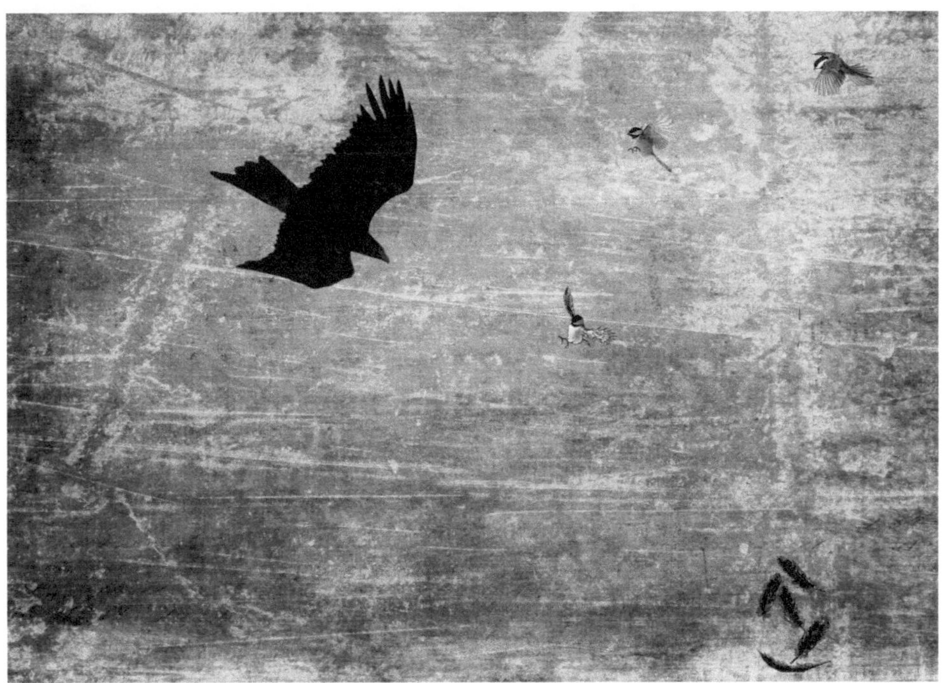

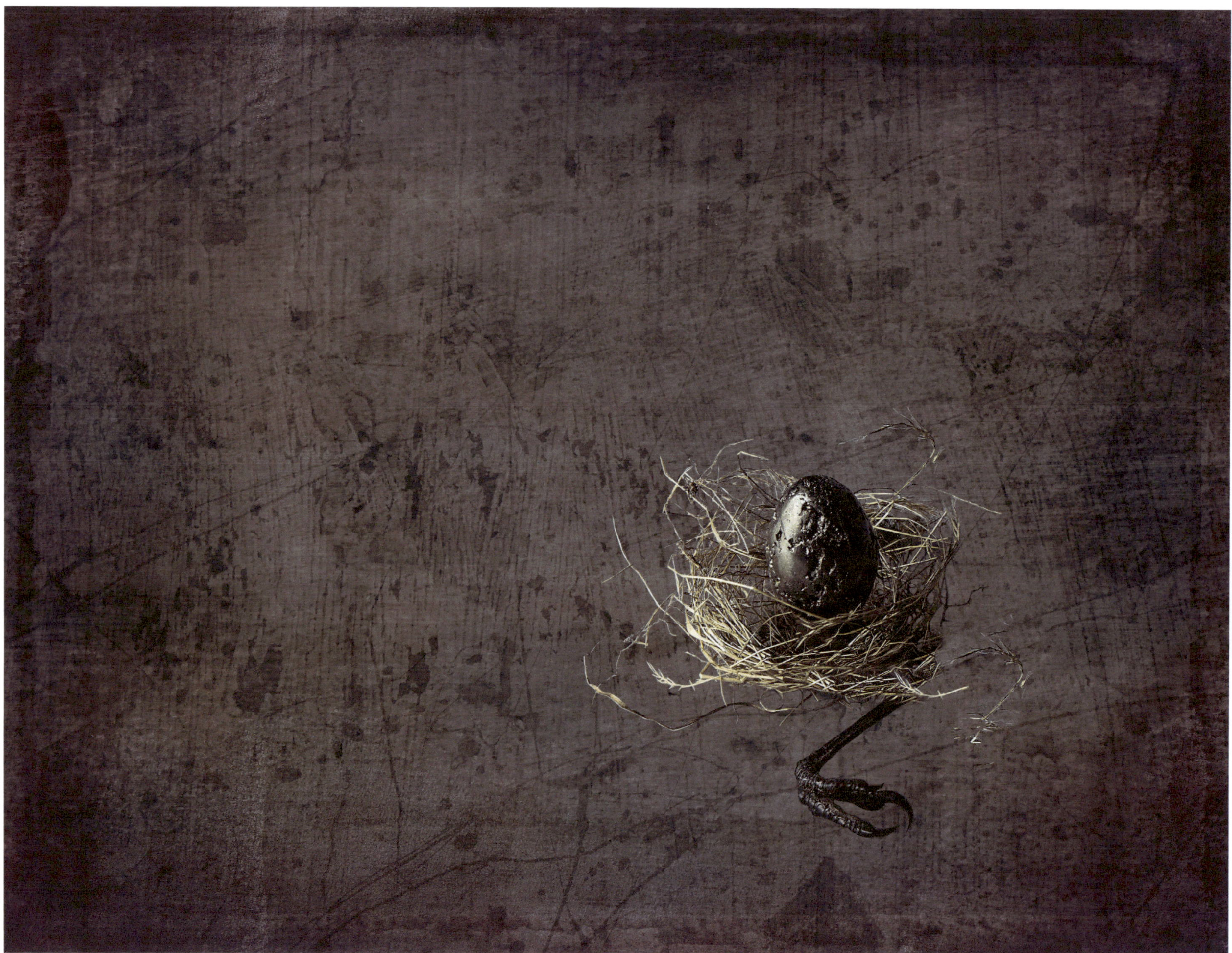

Witness...

We will survive
New care lines etch
our faces
...our hearts
A slight tremor shake
the once steady hand
We will survive
Pain will rule us for a while
Memories, newly crease
a tremulous smile
But we will survive
for that is what it is to grieve
There may be
disbelief
anger
denial
loss...
We witnessed
...we remain
in semblance, alive
and for her sake
we will survive
...until it is our time to leave

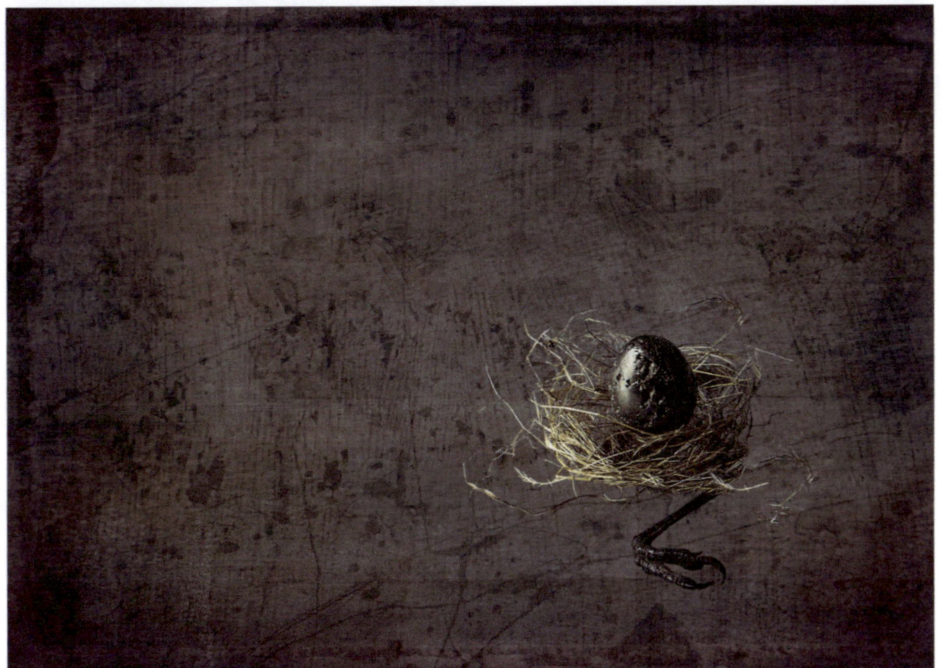

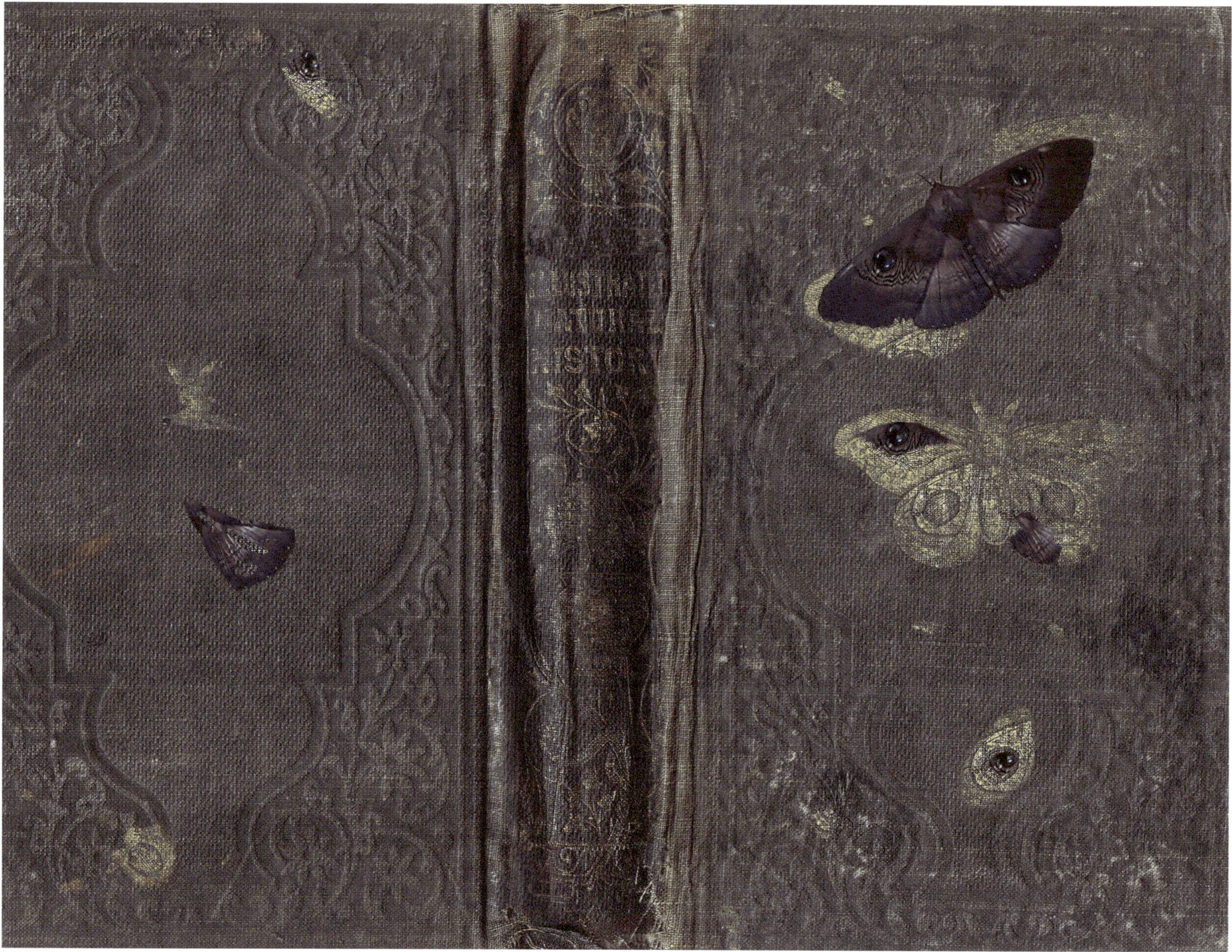

Dissolving...

What beats my heart
if not the drums of life
What kills my soul
if not war and strife
If I am gone
who mourns
the empty carcass, bare
If I disappear
what fills
the time-warped void
left there
The me I was
dissolving
Who gives a damn, then
it has no knowledge
left to share
We are all commodities
in each others lives
Food, water
shelter from a storm
that hapless drives
...until
the surface of this world
is wiped clean of man
and this troubled place
begins again
Empty
Dissolving
Reforming
...as it once began

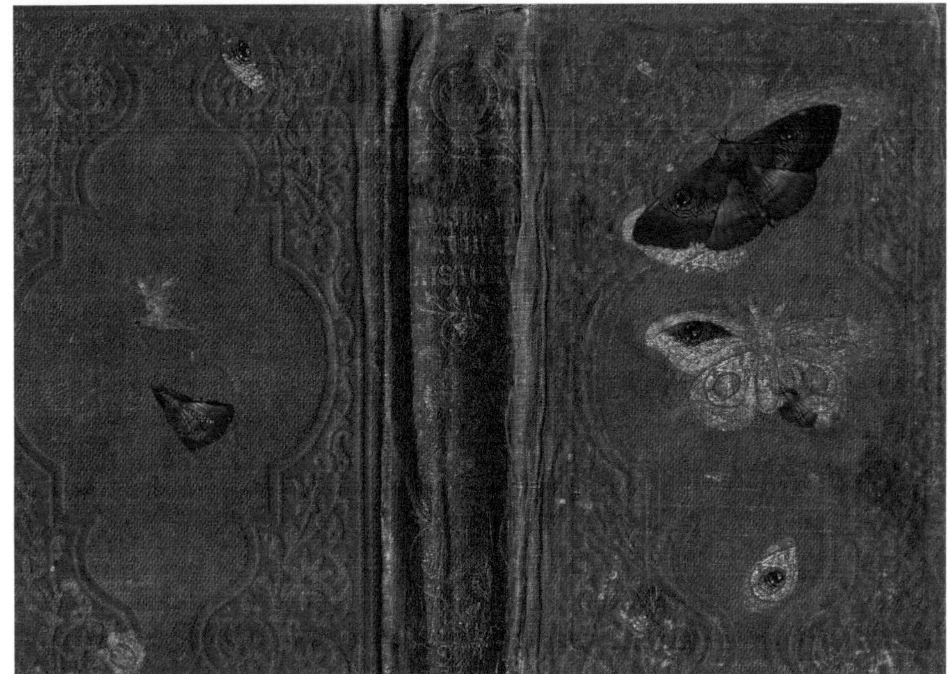

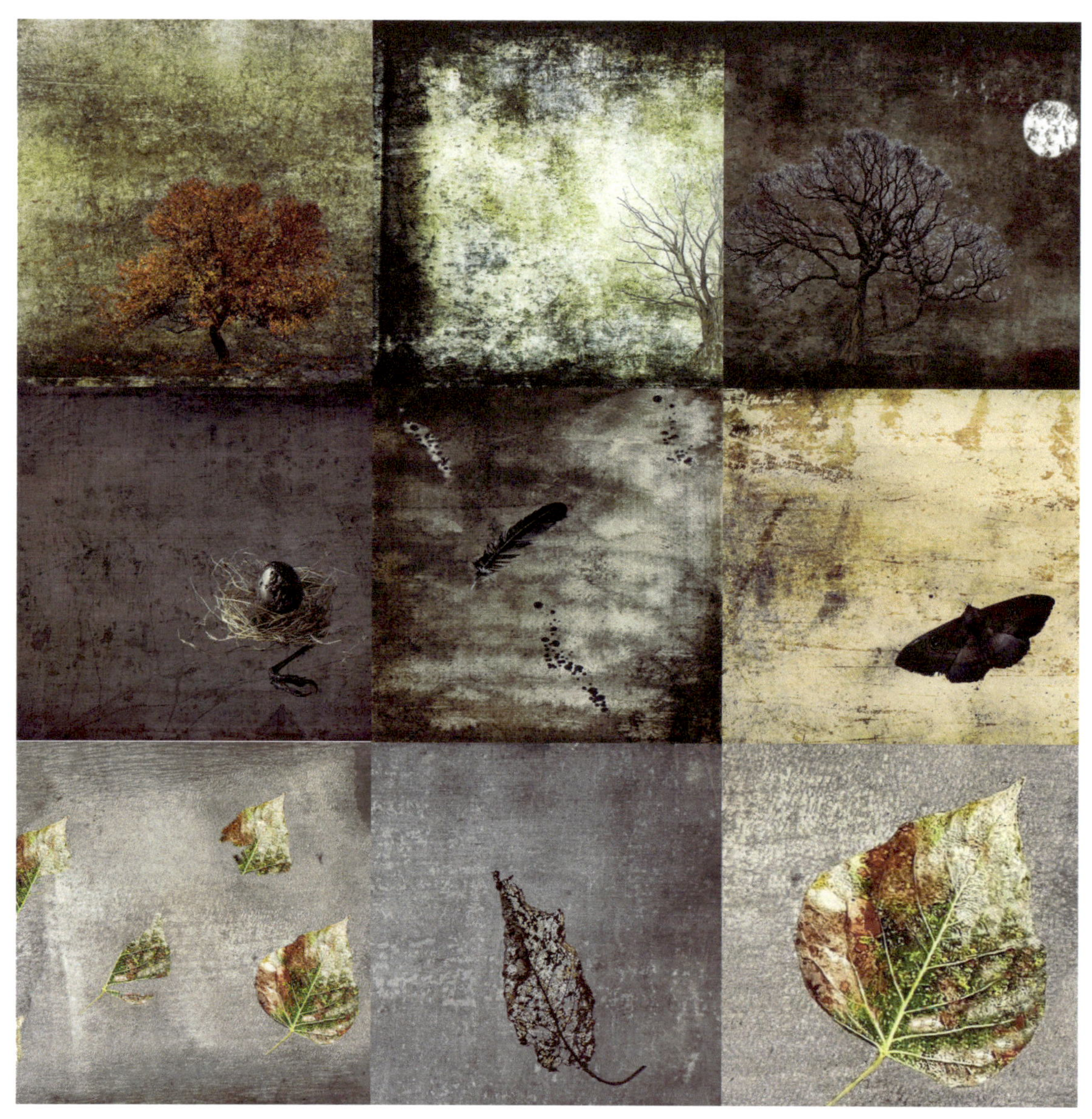

...a tapestry of discarded things that now, in stillness sings... of eternal flight. PR 2019

In Stillness...

The collection, In Stillness, was created through my daily immersion in nature after the sudden death of my eldest daughter. Each day a renewal occurs, within the natural cycles, from dawn to dusk, season to season, one moon cycle to the next and one solar year, to another.

Life can hand out raw and unexpected deals at times, but for me, it's important to continue trusting that all emotions pass, leaving bitter-sweet memories of previous times.

Visual references to the pain and loss we suffer, losses we experience, hone us as human beings, helping us to move closer to the planet as an intrinsic part of it, rather than separate, or overlord, to it.

All we have known is reflected in nature. We can draw from all the death and loss seen every day, so much of which goes unnoticed by the average, busy person, unless it falls within their own sphere of existence, but each day, a bird may fall from a nest, be storm-blown into unfamiliar landscapes or die, unknown and unmourned. We deem these, seemingly, *natural* occurrences, to be less important than a human death. Our grief and loss, apparently, far outweigh a fallen bird... but is this truly so?

By bearing witness to nature's losses, we can better understand, and mourn, our own personal, and collective, tragedies.

In Stillness, in gratitude... Penny Reilly 2019

Penny Reilly
107 Vincent Steet
Daylesford Victoria 3460
Australia
beyondthegategallery@hotmail.com

www.pennyreilly/wix.com
www.etsy.com/shop/BeyondthegateByPenny
www.facebook.com/beyondthegategallery
www.facebook.com/authoratbeyondthegatefarm
www.goodreads.com/pennyreilly
www.instagram.com/pennybeyondthegate
www.amazon.com/pennyreilly

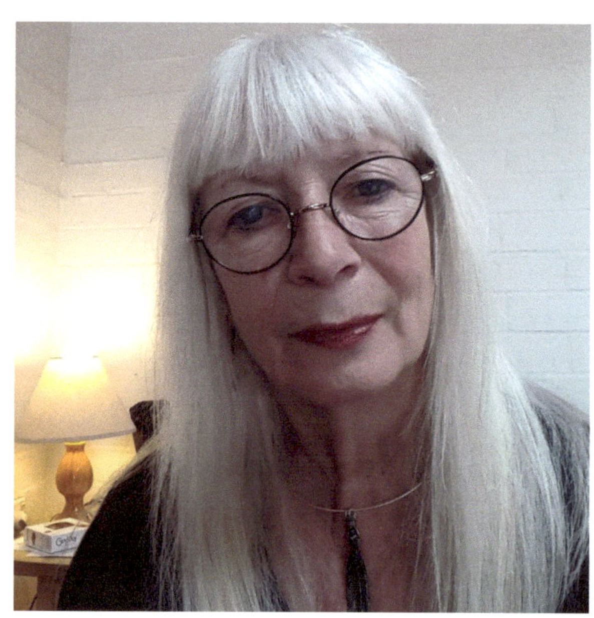

www.ingramcontent.com/pod-product-compliance
Lightning Source LLC
Chambersburg PA
CBHW042029050726

47599CB00005B/844